# PAULSON
# ON
# CHANGE

Make Change Work...
Thanks for Making a Difference!

Terry J. Paulson

The Grifffin Distilled Wisdom Series
Griffin Publishing

**First Edition 1996**
**10 9 8 7 6 5 4 3 2 1**

**ISBN1-882180-49-6**

**Griffin Publishing books are available at quantity discounts with bulk purchase for education, business, or sales promotional use. Contact Publishing Specials Sales by writing or fax.**

**Published by**
**Griffin Publishing**
**544 West Colorado Street**
**Glendale California 91204**
**(818) 244-2128 (818) 242-1172 Fax**
**Manufactured in the United States of America**

# PAULSON ON CHANGE

In today's changing business climate, what separates great leaders from the rest is the ability to translate their vision, values, and goals in ways that can be embraced by their teams. Motivation originates with an inner attitude, grows in response to shared goals, and endures as an energizing influence when reinforced through repeated exposure to insightful ideas. I trust that you will find the journey through the ideas in this book to be engaging, entertaining, and empowering to you and your team. Hopefully, you will be inspired by the quotes and struggle with the challenges they provide. Occasionally, you may even laugh at the universal humanness that the commentary exposes. The *right quotation* can open new windows into the world of business and the challenge of leadership. The *right insight* can be mined for best practices that will make your team's journey more productive. The *right question* can help you focus your own introspection and help you stimulate discussions with other members of your team. I've tried to provide all *three*. Welcome to the challenge of keeping hope alive in this age of unprecedented opportunity.

Terry L. Paulson, PhD, CSP, CPAE

## 1

*We want to think about global competition as if it's the Super Bowl. We want to play hard for the season, win the big game, and sit around during the off-season and gloat about how great we are. But the competitors we face in business today don't want to wait until next year for a rematch—they want to play again next week and every week until they finally win. It's tough for us to accept that we don't control the rules of the game anymore. We've got to be ready to battle formidable competitors everyday, forever, without a break.*

*—Bill Almon*

For the modern organization change occurs rapidly and continuously. It's tempting to say that soon we will be through this, but instead we must embrace the change journey as a never-ending opportunity.

What are you doing to prepare your team for a never ending race where you have to fix flat tires while moving?

## 2

*I hate bosses who distance themselves
from people. We have no secrets here.
So what if information gets to the
competition? The organization can
only be as good as the amount of
information shared among people.*
—*Karl Krapek*

Without information there is no empowerment. Instead of reporting outdated information on a *needs to know* basis, try sharing everything you can as early as possible unless you can specify a clear reason not to. If you do not give them accurate information on a timely basis, they will make up their own.

What information do your people need to do their job on a timely basis? What are you doing to make sure your people are working on the truth instead of wasting time on rumors?

*3*

*Business is essentially a game—one, moreover, that almost anyone can learn to play. As with most games, however, people won't bother to learn it unless they get it. That means, first, they must understand the rules; second, they must receive enough information to let them follow the action; and third, they must have the opportunity to win or lose. That's exactly how this company is run.*
*— Bo Burlingham*

People will work to win when they have a way to keep score. Don't wait until the end of the year to tell your team they lost. Let them know the numbers weekly while there is still something they can do to make a bottom-line difference.

What can you do to keep important results visible to your team?

*4*

*The most unproductive time we have is when we sit at our desks. Because the only thing we do is read history: what has already happened, what we cannot do anything about. When we leave our offices and start to walk around and talk to people, that's when we make things happen. You give your thoughts; you get thoughts back; you draw conclusions; perhaps you even make decisions.*

*—Jan Carlzon*

You can't manage change in a people business from your office. Computers and desks are seductive, but dangerous hiding places for managers who want to avoid real change. Change masters wander the halls enough to stay connected with the people they need to influence.

If you consider your people your most valuable asset, what proof would your people find by looking at how you invest your time?

*5*

*Lack of planning on your part does not constitute a crisis on my part.*

*—Sign used by Peter Ueberroth during the 1984 Olympics in Los Angeles*

Changing smart means honoring the call for *no surprises*. Use the 4 x's Rule—"For every unit of time you may be late, give four times the warning to all involved."

Are there *red flags* on the horizon warning you of pending problems that you haven't dealt with on a timely basis?

### 6

*Many companies are attracted by a fantasy version of empowerment and simultaneously repelled by the reality. How lovely to have energetic, dedicated workers who always seize the initiative (but only when 'appropriate'), who enjoy taking risks (but never risky ones), who volunteer their ideas (but only brilliant ones), who solve problems on their own (but make no mistakes), who aren't afraid to speak their minds (but never ruffle any feathers), who always give their very best to the company (but ask no unpleasant questions about what the company is giving them back). How nice it would be...to empower workers without actually giving them any power.*
—Peter Kizilos

$T$oo many workers are tired of hearing about *empowerment*. They want to drop the word and experience the reality. They want the information, the training, the resources, the clear boundaries and the rewards that come with making a difference.

What are you doing to make empowerment more than a slogan?

*7*

*I am convinced that if the rate of change inside an organization is less than the rate of change outside, the end is in sight.*
—*Jack Welch, Jr.*

When you embark on the change journey, don't expect to drop anchor. In fact, on a constantly moving ship, anchors left in the water are not helpful.

Are you on board, and what are you doing to keep even those that disagree on board with you?

### 8

*I solemnly promise and declare that every customer that comes within ten feet of me, I will smile, look them in the eye, and greet them, so help me Sam.*

*—Sam Walton's Wal-Mart Pledge*

Sam Walton worked the Wal-Mart mantra by leading employees in company cheers—"Give me a W! Give me an A! Give me an L! Give me a squiggly!..." You, too, can risk being corny for market-driven change. Too many people have confused professionalism with terminal seriousness.

What can you do to risk being corny in driving the vision and values of your organization?

### 9
*There is no limit to what you can accomplish if you don't care who gets the credit.*
*—Leslie G. McGraw, Jr..*

Effective leaders give more than
their share of the credit and take
more than their share of the blame.

What are you doing to make sure
that the right people are getting the
credit for making change work?

*10*
*My first message is: Listen, listen,*
*listen to the people who do the work.*
*—H. Ross Perot*

Make a habit of asking questions
that support your change efforts:
What are you doing differently?
What's working for you? What have
you learned that we could all
benefit from? What could we
provide our customers that they
are not yet aware that they need?

What other questions would you
add to this list?

*11*

*The man who doesn't read good
books has no advantage over the man
who can't read them.*
*—Mark Twain*

Training doesn't just come in expensive seminars. Take the time to read books as a team and discuss what you find. Take time to focus on books that can make a difference.

What book have you read lately that would be worth applying together as a team?

*12*

*We ask of our leaders what a child asks at bedtime: Tell me a story. As great historians and great leaders all know, narrative has power; stories define a nation.... Americans know their history through stories—Pocahontas and the first Thanksgiving, Washington's cherry tree and Lincoln's split rails. Our greatest politicians have traced the narrative lines out of our past and into the future.*

*—Michael Barone*

Leaders tell stories of their own to help us understand where we've come from and where we can be headed. Every culture has its heroes; wise leaders learn how to use them to set the stage for change.

What legendary stories from your organization can you use to help move your people confidently into the future?

### 13

*If you already are in the 'obsolete' category, surprise your manager by developing your own recovery program before he or she is forced to do it under much less favorable conditions.*

*—Dave Bowman*

Commitment to the individual often gets confused with an invitation to adoption and entitlement. Today, there is no such thing as business as usual. Job security comes with willingness to change and learn.

What are you doing to make sure your people are not left with skills nobody wants or needs?

### 14

*People in every nook and cranny of the organization are empowered—encouraged in fact—to do things their way. Suggestions are actively sought. But this all takes place within a context of direction. People know what the boundaries are; they know where they should act on their own and where not. The boss knows that his or her job is to establish the boundaries, and then truly get out of the way.*

*— Robert Waterman*

To Waterman, empowerment is best described as *directed autonomy*. Without boundaries or a strategic focus, empowerment is anarchy. With adequate thought to strategic direction and groundrules, leaders can nurture team confidence and develop trust in the team's effectiveness.

What have you done to let your people know what is out-of-bounds and where they can play the game of business with a minimum of interference?

*15*

*We found in the '80's that becoming faster is tied to becoming simpler. Our businesses, most with tens of thousands of employees, will not respond to visions that have sub-paragraphs and footnotes. If we're not simple we can't be fast..., and if we can't be fast, we can't win.*
*— Jack Welch, Jr.*

P eople need fast-moving central
driving ideas that can be
remembered and valued, but can
still evolve to sustain focus through
continually changing circumstances.

How would you tell someone in
two minutes what the values and
vision of your organization are?

*16*

*Place a bulletin board in each company restroom. When something needs to be communicated quickly to just about everyone, place the news on the bulletin board.*

*— Karen Herzog*

Getting through to people is more than newsletters and posters—it's finding new and creative ways to get information to people in ways that they will actually read it.

What are you doing to get through to your people the information they need to know?

## 17

*Never forget...that the most difficult thing in doing good business is to say no to bad business, the bad opportunities.... You must always decide who your customer is...and you should say no to every option that is not related to that customer's need.*
—*Jan Carlzon*

It takes just as much time to serve *bad business* as it does to serve *good business*. Don't just focus on what business comes your way; go after the business that will position you and your organization for expanded future opportunities.

What have you done to help your people know what *good business* is?

*18*

*The most senior people and virtually
all of the chief executive officers with
whom I'm personally acquainted
have highly developed senses of
humor. Humor is a common thread
I've seen in thousands of meetings in
different companies on the most
serious of subjects. Humor helps you
to keep your head clear when you're
dealing in highly technical
information or difficult decisions
where choices aren't that clear.*
—Don Seibert

Effective leaders know how to keep work fun. Don't walk the halls with your face "in park" unless you want to start rumors of layoffs.

What are you doing to take your job and mission seriously, but yourself lightly?

### 19

*Search out the energy and go where the energy is. It's similar to caring for a plant. You look for where the plant is beginning to flourish and then reallocate resources from dying branches toward the points of energy. Find people who already manifest what you want and find out how they are doing it. Then make them an example, give them more visibility, and start looking for more energy.*
—Gloria Regalbuto

Let the commitment of your people be as contagious as yours. Look for ways to feel, hear, and touch the power of empowerment at close range. Energetic, active listening is one of the best ways to communicate support and reflect back and fuel the enthusiasm you find in your team. To spread the good news to others, try increasing your positive gossip of what you find.

What are you doing to find and use the pockets of enthusiasm for change?

## 20

*The illiterate of the future are not those who cannot read or write, but those who cannot learn, unlearn, and relearn.*
—*Alvin Toffler*

Now is not the time to be good at a skill that no one needs. True security for employees comes with having skills that continue to add value. Insecure employees with outdated skills become frightened employees that are hard to motivate. Frightened employees vehemently fight change. Only employees with multiple skills have the options to be truly open to a rapidly changing future.

What are you doing to keep you and your team flexible, trained, and ready to add value to your customers' future?

*21*

*If you aren't having fun in your work, fix the problem before it becomes serious; ask for help if you need it. If you can't fix it and won't ask for help, please go away before you spoil the fun for the rest of us.*

*—Russ Walden*

Making change work doesn't have to be a terminally serious process. Laughter keeps the stress of deadlines in perspective, increases creativity in brainstorming, and helps bring teams together in a positive way. Take your job seriously, but yourself lightly.

What could you do today to bring the gift of laughter to your team?

*22*

*A change facilitator
provides...multiple paths. They keep
five or six streams running and
make sure new streams come along
so that branching continues. A
change facilitator is someone who is
looking not for closings but for
openings. We can't control change.
That's not the issue anymore. It is
managing the ride, rolling with the
flow. That is very different from
where we've been and not a place
where we are comfortable. It involves
a lot of risk.*
—Gloria Regalbuto

Any leader that says they have a crystal-clear vision of the future is either uninformed or lying. Successful leaders must provide a compelling direction that fosters action and allows for discovery on the road to the future. They capitalize on the surprise, adventure, and flexibility that is inherent in the change process. Do your part to paint a focused and compelling vision of the future, but let your teams be the scouts that find the right path and map out the details as they move.

What are you doing to encourage innovative openings to your vision of the future?

### 23

*The situation becomes downright comical when a company run by a group of multimillion-dollar executives begins to espouse the popular (and convenient) theory that today's employees are not especially motivated by money. The 'new worker' would much rather have lots of (free) praise and (inexpensive) motivational pamphlets and (cheap) little heart-shaped lapel pins that tell the world she did a swell job of waiting on a customer. Presumably, the only people left in America for whom money is a primary motivator are CEOs, stockholders and dishwashers in Reno.*
—Jack Gordon

It's time that all on the team
participate in the fruits of victory
and share in the cost of setbacks.

As the age of entitlement and
lifelong employment slips away,
what are you doing to change the
reward system to support the
people who are making change
work?

*24*

*In an empowered organization there
are bound to be a lot more
disagreements. Because we value
open and direct communication, we
give people permission to disagree.*
*— Robert D. Haas*

Hidden problems become big problems, the kind that competitors exploit and *60 Minutes* shares with the world. In a changing organization, diversity and differences are not obstacles; they are two of an organization's principal strengths. Be known as a leader that encourages problem solving instead of problem evading.

What are you doing to promote healthy disagreements in your organization?

## 25

*Bored people are the most unhappy people in the world. They hate their jobs, and they complain about how lousy the company is, as demonstrated by the way it uses their time. People have to feel good about getting a paycheck. Otherwise, they look for a reason to level it in their own minds. You destroy character when you employ too many people to do a job. Busy people are happy people.*

—Ken Hendricks

The bar has been raised for all workers, but it is far too easy to burn out the best while adopting and avoiding the worst. Care enough to engage *all* of your workers, or the wrong workers will leave. Challenge the unmotivated, train them, and, if necessary, redirect them where their skills and passion can serve you...*or someone else*!

What are you doing to hold previously adopted and underutilized employees accountable?

*26*

*I want to make this plant 'inefficient.' I want to make it profitable. We thought of our factory as an efficiency machine. We had to see it as a profit center—to focus on opportunities for sales, rather than problems of cost. People expected to be judged on their own efficiency, on their process in isolation, apart from whether it made us money. I told them to think like baseball players. You never saw George Brett walk off the field a winner while the rest of the Royals lost. That's the goal in a nutshell.*

*—Martha Roberts*

Your goal is not to just cut overhead costs but to make your business more productive and responsive to your customers. Enthusiasm for efficiency remains important, but enthusiasm without focus can be costly. Such misdirected passion can take time and resources away from making a needed difference to a customer that is waiting to be served. Doing one's best is only important if it's something a customer wants.

What are you doing to keep your team's efforts focused on customer driven needs not *right way* reverence?

### 27

*All the analysis in the world will never generate a vision. Many who are qualified to lead fail to do so because they try to substitute analysis for vision. What they never grasp is that the natural energy for changing reality comes from holding a picture of what might be that is more important to people than what is.*
—*Peter M. Senge*

It's the tension between *what is* and *what can* be that inspires the drive that every change effort requires. No organization can analyze and shrink its way to greatness. Don't limit yourself to cost cutting and downsizing while your people are waiting for a direction that can give them hope for a profitable future.

What are you doing to paint pictures of a future vision worth achieving?

## 28

*Tell the truth. When people try to inspire employee commitment, they tend to sugar-coat harsh reality. It's better to tell the truth. Yes, it is difficult to tell employees that you'll probably be short-staffed indefinitely, that promotions are unlikely, and that overtime may be the norm for awhile. Doing so creates the possibility for partnership and true commitment.*

*— Ken Macher*

Trust is a fragile commodity that is important to maintain, easy to lose, and hard to win back. Selling the vision requires leaders that believe in their workers ability to accomplish their mission and also believe in giving honest, timely information about the obstacles people will need to overcome to make the vision a reality.

What are you doing to accomplish both?

### 29

*"I had a dream, I reached it. I lost the dream, and I miss it." It was the same for our whole organization. We had a dream and we reached it, and we reached it very quickly. It had all been a little too easy. And we created frustration, because this is a psychological game. Do you know the song Peggy Lee sings, 'Is That All Their Is?' I learned that, before you reach an objective, you must be ready with a new one, and you must start to communicate it to the organization.*

*—Jan Carlzon*

It's great to have a vision, but what happens when you get there? There is a need to celebrate victories, but there is also a pressing need for leaders to focus on new worlds yet to be discovered. Don't think of movies with endings; think of serials with never-ending plots worth developing.

What are you doing to keep the organizational dream new and alive?

### 30

*What's imperative is the creation of a style that becomes a culture. It may be forced, it may be designed. But the real sense of change, that anarchy—we need a department of surprises. Whatever we do, we have to preserve the sense of being different. We just have to make sure we won't wind up like an ordinary company.*

*— Anita Roddick*

Successful companies build surprise, adventure, and flexibility into the change process. They have strategic plans, but must do most of their planning in pencil with an eye towards multiple options. We used to be content searching for the right answer, now we're not even sure we're asking the right questions.

Who is taking care of the department of surprises for your organization?

*31*
*None of this is hard to understand.*
*None of it is easy to do. Change is*
*threatening. There is no right way.*
*There is no learning without*
*mistakes.*
*—Mary Walton*

$P$art of any *Change Agent's Bill of Rights* ought to include the right to make mistakes without having to cover one's behind. To manage change, leaders must manage error. As soon as there is change, there is error. The job is not to prevent error, but to encourage as many early mistakes as possible to promote learning, surface problems, insure consistent quality by the time the product or service ever reaches the customer.

What are you doing to make early errors a learning experience instead of an invitation to procrastination and paralysis?

*32*

*IBM would have gone into Chapter 11 if it didn't have enough good people who were afraid to leave.*
*—Daniel Burrus*

$F$ind the *teachable moments* and use them. *Teachable moments* come when people are aware of a big enough reason for the work of change to seem a small price to pay for survival. With any luck you won't have to wait until you go into Chapter 11. Try generating motivation before disaster strikes by using the misfortune of others. Share frequently examples of companies from related industries that waited too long to make changes and suffered an untimely demise or a painful restructuring .

What *teachable moments* could you use to help energize the change process?

*33*

*There is a tremendous capability for anarchy if people do their own thing. The way you avoid that is to be very...clear about why we all got together in the first place. We have a focused mission. It's that clarity that allows us to stretch out and do a lot of different things. I sometimes describe this as a cable-car ride. Cable cars have those bars on the sides that you can hang onto and lean way out. You can try all sorts of things, but you've got to have the bar or you fall off.*

—*John Rollwagen*

Encouraging workers to be innovative and to take risks may generate more problems than profitable opportunities. It's not the number of ideas generated that is important; it is whether the focus of the innovations adds value to the customers you serve. Encourage innovation, but keep them focused where it counts.

What are you doing to provide the strategic direction, the limits, and the support that allows your people to stretch their thinking into new answers to meet your customers' needs?

### 34

*My competitors...want people under their thumb. I don't. I want systems in place. I want people who can figure out a better way and let me know what it is, so we can improve on what we've got. I'm trying to create entrepreneurs. My competitors are looking for more and more control. That's why I have no fear of their stealing my secrets. I really don't have any secrets. Everything I do is basic business.*

*—Ken Hendricks*

What is a priceless, well-protected secret today, is a commodity tomorrow. Only in open systems can you establish the speed and flexibility your organization needs to create new secrets that will insure your continued success.

What are you doing to develop and take advantage of an entrepreneurial spirit within your organization?

### 35

*If there is any lesson to be drawn
from the past two decades of
American Business, it is that assets
are transitory. The assets you created
yesterday are already declining in
value because of changing customer
needs, evolving technology, and
increased competition. The question
isn't whether your products or
services will become obsolete. It isn't
even when. You can absolutely count
on the fact that they will become
obsolete soon. The only question is
whether they will be replaced by
someone else's products or your own.*
—George Gendron

In this age of chaotic change and global competition, one of the best predictors of bankruptcy may be a good year. Too many corporate celebrations take a wrong turn into complacency. A good year should foster leadership that invests the fruits of success into relistening to customers and retooling their troops with the skills that it will take to meet future customer needs. Surprises are always hard to handle, but if the surprises come from your competition, it may mean your survival. Don't wait until you're sick to mount a comeback.

What are you doing to turn short-term successes into a dynasty that lasts?

*36*

*Give me the laziest man you can find. I will put him in the hardest area I've got in the warehouse. And in two weeks he'll have it running smooth. Why? Because he's lazy. He's not going to work hard. He'll do it the first day the hard way. The second day, he'll think about it.*
—Rodney King

Have you raised the bar for all your people, or are you settling for burning out *only* your best? When most managers believe that certain people are incapable of change, they work around them instead of through them.

What are you doing to make sure that all team members feel the challenge of change?

*37*

*People ask about skeptics, and it's always in a negative way. But I think the skeptics help bring the champions back to reality. I need that. I can get off on a target very quickly.*
—Charles Caldwell

Not every change is an improvement. Sometimes those who resist are right. When one person calls you a horse's behind, don't worry. But when four people do, go out and buy a saddle!

Where has resistance worked for you in avoiding a costly mistake? Over what decisions should you buy a saddle?

### 38

*Many companies have given up on participative management when the heat was on. That is exactly the time you ought to depend upon it most. I think you have to believe some very difficult things to make it work for a long time. It is not a theoretical position to be adopted after reading a few journals. You have to believe in the potential of people. Participative management without a belief in that potential and without convictions about the gifts that people bring to organizations is a contradiction of terms.*

*—Max De Pree*

While going through change, don't just dabble in participative management; live by it by keeping teams involved when the times get tough. If group decision making is the strategy of choice in the good times, it is even more important to stay with it when the pressure is on.

Where could you rely more effectively on your team?

### 39

*If front-line employees are actually to make decisions that entail some risk, they must have a sense of security. Having knowledge and information is not enough if they believe a wrong decision may cause them problems or even the loss of their job. They must know that they are allowed to make mistakes. Only then will they dare to use fully their new authority.*

*—Jan Carlzon*

Learn to support heroic efforts even when mistakes produce less than ideal results. With movement comes error. When leaders overreact, workers hide errors or resist change. When teams are allowed to learn early from errors, the quality pursuit of perfection becomes possible. By taking the heat for early errors instead of blaming your team, they will be secure enough to commit to making quality change work for the long haul.

What heroic efforts do you need to be visibly supporting?

*40*

*Our role as leaders is not to catch people doing things wrong but to create an environment in which people can become heroes.*

*—Newt Hardie*

Most managers major in looking for problems to overcome, not victories to celebrate. Do your part in making sure that today's heroes and high-functioning teams in your organization are found, seen, honored, and used in sustaining the change journey.

What heroes have you caught this week? How could you positively gossip about their effectiveness?

### 41

*Be yourself. Figure out what you're good at. Hire only people who care. Treat them just the way you want to be treated. Switch from macho to maestro. Identify your one or two key objectives or directions. Ask your co-workers how to get there. Listen hard. Get out of their way. Cheer them. Count the gains. Start right now.*

*—Warren Bennis*

$W$hy be complex, when you can keep leadership simple. Read this summary daily and get busy putting your calendar where your vision is.

What would you put in your leadership short course?

*42*
*There has been an alarming increase*
*in the number of things I know*
*nothing about.*
*—Ashleigh Brilliant*

No leader needs to know it all, but you had better know *something* worth knowing. Don't wait for people to tell you that you are obsolete. Invest in learning something new every day. You become an old dog when you stop doing new tricks.

What new tricks have you been learning?

### 43

*Once people start not knowing the people in the building and it starts to become impersonal, it's time to break up a company. I'd say that number is around 50 or 60 people. By keeping it small, you give more people a chance. A company operates at its peak when people are able to know each other's strengths and weaknesses. I don't want people to get lost in the corridors of power.*
—*Richard Branson*

$\mathbf{D}$on't just grow big to live someone else's image of success. Be small enough to stay effective, flexible, and empowered.

At whatever size, what can you do to keep your company working small?

### 44
*I'm like a periscope for the rest of the company. Nobody gets to see it and the world from exactly my vantage point, so I try to spread that around.*
— *John Rollwagen*

Creating a vision requires painting a picture of what profitable destinations you see on the horizon and what course corrections may be necessary to get there. The motivation to move into the future can't come from the past; it comes from a compelling future vision that inspires the commitment of managers and workers alike.

Do your people know what you see in the periscope? Are they excited by what you see?

*45*
*Hire smart people even in areas
where it's not clear to you why you
need such broad and smart people.
Hire people who really have the
energy level and the commitment to
persevere through inevitable disaster
periods and see beyond them.*
*— Bill Gates*

It's the people, stupid! The best hardware and software marvels of the week have guaranteed obsolescence built in; at best, they have a half-life that can be measured in days. In the information age, it's the people that make the difference—their flexible skills, their ability to work as a team, and their passionate commitment to make change work over and over again.

If you *were* forming a new company, which of your people bring the passion and the skills that would make you hire them anew? If you wouldn't choose some, why are they still there?

*46*

*The last thing you want to do is reward people out of their jobs. If a work team is bright enough to figure out a way to reduce the number of people they need, and we don't have an opening somewhere else, we'll tell the extra workers to go think about other improvements.*

*— Fred Wenninger*

You will never build the future by cutting costs; you build the future by freeing up good people to capture the wealth and opportunity that is on the move in our changing global economy. Instead of making people invest time worrying about losing their job because you can't afford them, free them to look for ways they can add bottom-line revenue so you can't afford to lose them. Being lean and mean is not a strategy for the future. Instead of defending dying empires on a crash diet, let your people conquer new territory.

What are you doing to become more than champions of the status quo?

*47*

*The role is marked by involvement more than by telling....We say to chief executive officers: Paint the picture, paint the vision, preach the story. At the same time, remember that listening and involvement are the ways that you'll pull it off.*
*—Tom Peters*

Listening makes listeners. The biggest difference between being enthusiastic and generating enthusiasm is whose ideas you get excited about. Leaders don't just talk values; they *live their values*.

What are you doing to listen long enough to find examples of what you value in the actions and ideas of your people?

*48*
*Do what you can, with what you have, where you are.*
—*Theodore Roosevelt*

In the real world, you don't control the cards you are dealt, but you do control the choices you make in playing the cards in your hand. There is never *nothing* you can do. There is *always* a question as to whether it will work and whether it is worth the investment of time involved. Keep working the *3 P's— Position, Perform, Persist. Position* for opportunity, work at constantly improving your *performance*, and *persist* in doing it again in a world of constant change.

What choices do you need to make in playing your current hand?

*49*

*People only change when confronted with strong leadership, crisis, or both. Therefore, unless you are willing to be at the whim of crises, strong leadership is the only reliable change force you have.*
—*Thomas C. Gibson*

Too many companies and their leaders wait until they are sick to take a costly cure that almost always costs workers jobs. When companies wait for a crisis to be a catalyst for change, they seldom have the money or time to do it well. Try a new strategy; try not getting sick. Be the first on the block to not need a comeback. Try learning from the failure of others instead of waiting for your own. Bring in articles for your people to read about organizations that waited too long to change. Just don't try to change people until they buy the *need to change*.

What are you doing to generate an awareness of the need to change while you still have the time and the resources to make change work?

### 50

*I never hesitated to promote someone
I didn't like. The comfortable
assistant, the nice guy you like to go
on fishing trips with, is a great
pitfall. Instead I looked for those
sharp, scratchy, harsh, almost
unpleasant guys who see and tell you
about things as they really are. If you
can get enough of them around you
and have patience enough to hear
them out, there is no limit to where
you can go.*
—*Thomas Watson, Jr.*

If everyone is so nice that they always agree with you, many of them are probably unnecessary. When you have people who care enough to confront you eyeball-to-eyeball, you won't have to wait until your customers tell you by buying from someone else.

What are you doing to make sure your people are disagreeable enough to tell you the truth you need to hear?

### 51

*Empowerment, the collective effect of leadership, is most evident in four themes: People feel significant. Learning and competence matter. People are a part of a community effort. Work is exciting.*
*—Warren Bennis*

$Y$ou can't make change work with people who are just *doing a job*. You need people who are willing to add value, to be lifelong learners, to make teams work, and to be passionately excited about making the organization's vision a reality.

As a leader, what are you doing to recognize, support, train, pay, and empower those workers that are doing just that?

*52*

*The more you motivate people, the
more they want to interact with you. I
started Deli Days in 1988. They are
held a few days each month. If you
want to see me, you take a number
from a ticket wheel outside my office.
Above it is an electronic numbers
board ("Now Serving"), which I
control with a switch under my desk.
The idea is that you take a number
and wait until it pops up on the
board. Each person has five or six
minutes to talk with me about
anything he or she wants. I think the
most important rule, regardless of
where you work, is to be honest with
the people who work for you. You
can't come off like a guru who knows
everything and doesn't have a single
flaw. But you can be a manager who
creates an environment in which
new ideas are encouraged and
rewarded.*
—Katherine Hudson

Everyone knows the importance of listening; few do it well. In a world of information overload and crowded calendars, time to listen is one of the first priorities to fall by the wayside. After all, as managers we have important things to do and say. Unfortunately, if you're not listening, you're not leading. Try developing a new habit by scheduling time to listen to your people every week.

What questions would you ask to define your focus as a listening leader?

### 53

*I have learned how to hold a team together. How to lift some men up, how to calm down the others, until finally they've got one heartbeat together, a team. There's just three things I'd ever say: If anything goes bad, I did it. If anything goes semi-good, then we did it. If anything goes real good, then you did it. That's all it takes to get people to win football games for you.*

*—Bear Bryant*

Recognition and acknowledgment are the accelerator pedals of change. Micromanaging and misdirected blaming are the brake pedals.

Which pedals are you riding in your pursuit of change?

The Distilled Wisdom Series

*54*

*In times of rapid change, experience
could be your worst enemy.*
—*J. Paul Getty*

Every improvement is the result of change; not every change is an improvement. The past will always have value, but it can't have a veto. The best companies are open to any change that improves, but are also willing to hold on to any legacy or tradition that passes the test of time.

What are you doing to help your people search for and appreciate the valuable lessons that both the past and the future have to offer?

*55*
*Why did I choose a tenfold*
*improvement as a goal? Because I*
*wanted to force people to view their*
*jobs in a different way. The*
*magnitude of the challenge changed*
*the way people in R & D and*
*manufacturing viewed each other. It*
*forced people to work across*
*organizational boundaries.*
*—John Young*

Comfortable workers rest in comfortable strategies. Comfortable leaders lulled by comfortable numbers often let teams settle for comfortable results until competitors force them to change under *much less* comfortable conditions. Comfortable companies are vulnerable to hungry, uncomfortable competitors. Good leaders know how to make their own people uncomfortable enough to make changes happen before they are forced to do so by customers that stop buying.

What are you doing to make your people uncomfortable enough to explore uncharted territory in pursuit of new more profitable routes and unfound treasures?

*56*
*Only when your aspirations and desires lie outside your resources does creativity occur, because you have to invent new ways of competing and change the rules of the game.*
—*C. K. Prahalad*

Make your strategic challenge a stretch instead of an incremental step. Don't scale down your ambitions; people are inspired to be innovative when you expand their horizons out of their comfort zone.

What are you doing to challenge your team to think outside the envelope?

### 57

*Post-heroic leaders don't expect to solve all the problems themselves. They realize no one person can deal with the emerging and colliding tyrannies of speed, quality, customer satisfaction, innovation, diversity, and technology. Virtual leaders say no to their egos. They are confident enough in their vision to delegate true responsibility, both for the tedium of process and for the sweep of strategic planning. And they are careful to "model," or live by, the values they espouse.*
*—John Huey*

The age where leaders were promoted for knowing all the answers is over. Now they have the wisdom to hire the best people they can, know the limitations of their own knowledge, and know how to orchestrate and thrive on team victories.

What are you doing that you ought to be delegating?

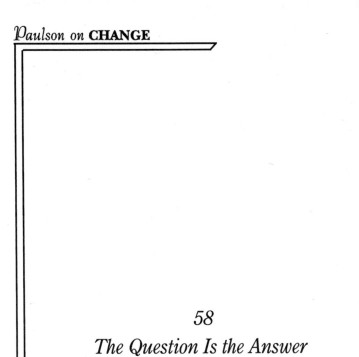

*58*

*The Question Is the Answer*

*—A sign on the desk of Ralph Stayer*

Leaders seem to love to give answers, and workers seem somehow relieved to receive them. But today's best empowering leaders resist the role of resident *answer giver*! Sometimes just staying silent and giving no direction can be your best response. After a pause, learn to ask, "You've been thinking about this longer than I have, what do you suggest?"

Where are you leading with answers when you should be leading with the right questions?

*59*
*We teach collaborative problem-solving. In school that's called cheating.*
*—Edward Bales*

The age of the omnipotent leader that tells others how to be successful is over; we now need approachable, listening leaders that are ready to capitalize on the best ideas that surface in the pursuit of the organization's mission.

What are you doing to build and support a culture that collaboratively *cheats?*

## 60

*Leadership is a verb, not a noun.*
*Leadership is defined by what you*
*do, not who you are. Leaders are*
*those whom others follow.*
*—Bill Gore*

$B$ill Gore has built what he calls an *un-management* system for his company. No one holds titles, except as required for incorporation purposes. Nobody gets hired until a company associate agrees to "sponsor" the person which includes finding work for him or her.

Where are labels, boxes, and management perks getting in the way of change in your organization?

### 61

*The other thing I strongly believe in,
and without which so many people
fail, is focus. When you're growing a
business, there are so many things
that can attract you to the left or
right. Venture capitalists have new
ideas every 47 minutes. If you tried
to do even a tenth of them, you'd go
crazy.*

*—Robert Nourse*

You can't do it all and retain excellence. Focus on targeting your risk taking and quality efforts strategically. Position your people and your resources to make a difference where it counts for the customers or the people you serve.

Where are you wasting resources that could be redirected?

## 62

*American workers don't speak up because they fear being ostracized, cut off from the information flow. They aren't afraid of losing their job. They're afraid of the 'soft' repercussions, that they will in some way be shunned for pointing out a problem. In related research, fully 70 percent of workers didn't speak up to the people who could solve a problem. That means managers have an inadequate pool of information for making decisions. That, in turn, fuels workers' perceptions that managers aren't to be trusted.*

*—Joshua Hammond*

If 70% of American workers are afraid to speak up with suggestions or to ask for clarification, we have teams who are playing it safe at a time when organizations need the wild, far out, even wacko ideas, that will move them profitably into the future.

What are you doing to buffer the organizational immune system that attacks radical ideas, critical input, and unsettling questions?

## 63

*Managing diversity does not mean controlling or containing diversity, it means enabling every member of your work force to perform to his or her potential. It means getting from employees, first, everything we have a right to expect, and, second, if we do it well, everything they have to give.*
—R. Roosevelt Thomas, Jr.

Does a program, policy, or principle give special consideration to any one group? Will it contribute to everyone's success, or will it produce an advantage for blacks, whites, women, men or any particular group? Is it designed for *them* as opposed to *us*? Whenever the answer is *yes,* you're not yet on the road to making diversity work for change in your organization.

What are you doing to make sure that workers from all backgrounds and genders who are making a difference are visible as positive examples of how diversity adds value?

## 64

*Basically, what you end up with is some PR statement that's put on a wall and called a mission statement. There's very little emotional buy-in. The second reason mission statements don't work is that organizations don't use them as constitutions. The key to a mission statement is that it should be used every day. It should represent the frame of reference by which every decision is made. It is not a boss-centered environment, it is a principle-centered environment, and everyone should participate in developing what those principles are.*
*—Stephen Covey*

There is value in having everyone contribute to establishing what *true north* is for your organization. If your people don't get that luxury, at least let them clarify and discuss what the mission statement and stated values mean to the decisions they have to make.

What are you doing on a weekly basis to get and keep your team focused on your organization's values?

## 65
*The first and last task of a leader is to keep hope alive.*
*— John W. Gardner*

Good leaders inspire people!
They find a hundred unique,
energizing ways to make their
vision live in the minds of their
people.

What are you doing to be a hope
merchant for positive change
within your organization?

### 66

*You have to have vision and a game plan of inclusion. You have to go slower rather than faster. And, finally, you have to hope for a scandal to create a reform-friendly climate.*
—*Meg Armstrong*

Good leaders don't wait for disasters or for scandals to mobilize change. Instead of waiting until drastic action is required, they use the disasters of others to help sell the need for change to their team. By generating the need for change early in the change process, leaders and their teams still have the revenue and the resources to make needed changes work.

What example of organizational failure could you use to communicate the potential cost of not changing?

### 67

*A change with a clear payoff for those who must do the changing will feel like a challenge. If it lacks such a payoff, it will feel like a burden.*
—*Clay Carr*

$A$re changes in your company a burden or a challenge? Ultimately, each team member must answer the question for herself, but leaders can help by providing the information that will make the need and the payoff for change evident.

What are you doing to communicate the payoff for change?

The Distilled Wisdom Series

*68*

*Don't look at automating what you're
doing. Look at why you're doing it
and whether you should do it at all.
Only then, look at the technology.*
—*Jim Grant*

Even embracing technological solutions can easily waste time on activity that no one or no computer should do. The operational fat in most organizations is marbled in, and you have to identify it before you can grind and fry it out. Don't ask, "Can it be done better with technology?" until you have first asked, "Is it worth doing at all?"

What are you doing to get rid of operational fat?

### 69

*In a command and control
organization, people protect
knowledge because it's their claim to
distinction. But we share as much
information as we possibly can
throughout the company. Business
literacy is a big issue in developing
leadership. You cannot ask people to
exercise broader judgment if their
world is bounded by very narrow
vision.*
—*Robert Haas*

Without information there is no empowerment. That which will eventually be revealed should be immediately revealed to allow early course corrections, effective team brainstorming, and empowered implementation at the lowest level possible.

What are you doing to get information into the hands of the people who need it most?

*70*
*Every person I work with knows something better than I. My job is to listen long enough to find it and use it.*
— *Jack Nichols*

$B$e a *listening leader.* Try taking a fifteen minute walk with every one of your direct reports once a week. Ask weekly, "What's working for you?" Listen to the answers and be ready to use the best ideas that surface.

What else would you want to consistently ask on your weekly walk?

### 71
*The expert at battle seeks his victory
from strategic advantage and does
not demand it from his men.*
*—General Sun Wu*

$R$ule #1: It's easiest to ride a horse in the direction it is going.

$R$ule #2: If the horse is dead, get off it.

$R$ule #3: Since it is hard to tell if your horse is dying, have at least two horses. In fact, in today's chaotic and constantly changing world, have a herd of horses!

What are you doing to add to your herd of horses?

## 72

*Never confuse activity with results.
You don't get points for predicting
rain. You get points for building
arks.*

*—Lou Gerstner, Jr.*

$W$hen people are adding value
and producing results, they want
*more than* points. Too many times,
when people build their arks, all
the only payment they receive is an
opportunity to clean all the cages.
Pay for production, not
predictions,...but pay!

What are you doing to align your
reward system to support
producing results instead of
entitlements?

## 73

*During the earthquake emergency, city employees adopted what I call the Riordan axiom—it's much easier to get forgiveness than to get permission. Just do it! Give people the power to make decisions, make mistakes, and correct mistakes and they will amaze you with what they can do.*

*—Richard Riordan*

When an empowered culture is working, even extreme conditions can provide opportunities to build trust and renewed commitment to accomplishing the mission of the organization.

What are you doing to free your people to act in support of the mission of your organization?

## 74

*We found that the most exciting environments, that treated people very well, are also tough as nails. There is no bureaucratic mumbo-jumbo... Excellent companies provide two things simultaneously: Tough environments and very supportive environments.*
—Tom Peters

Every leader must find a way to balance accountability with strong support. The best teachers expected a lot of you, would not settle for less than your best, provided tough but constructive feedback, and made you earn your good grade and their respect. Leaders cannot adopt some employees and burn out the best and expect to meet the challenge of change.

What are you doing to consistently challenge and support all of your people?

### 75

*If I was going to fix what I made, I would have to start by fixing myself. In many ways that was my good luck. Thank God I was the problem so I could be the solution.*
—*Ralph Stayer*

I'm sure that you can think of others that ought to take this quote to heart. Unfortunately, it's always easier to think of others that need to change than it is to face the fact that true change starts when you look in the mirror at the one person you truly control—yourself. Often the biggest single block to teams making needed changes resides in the leader's ability to change how he or she leads.

What are you doing as a leader to lead change starting with yourself?

# INDEX

## The Griffin Distilled Wisdom Series

Ever since the best selling *Life's Little Instruction Book*, there has been a growing supply of quotation books that give readers bite-sized doses of wisdom that stimulate, entertain, and enlighten. The Griffin Distilled Wisdom Series goes beyond the collection of stimulating quotations to provide today's leaders with practical and insightful commentary from the author and questions they can use to direct their own thoughts and the thoughts of their people. In today's world of global competition and revolutionary change, learning is a never-ending process. These books provide the ammunition you need to help you lead your organization into the 21st Century. In a matter of minutes, you can find the insights, the messages, and the questions you are looking for to reinforce the things that matter most to you and your organization.

Each book in the Griffin Distilled Wisdom Series is indexed by key content areas for easy access. Our goal is simple, to help you reach and reinforce your goals. May you find the series a source of new ideas to help your career, to build your business, and to improve your life. Enjoy all of the books in the series....

Paulson on Change
Paulson on Quality
Paulson on Humor
Sanborn on Success
Sanborn on Customer Service
Sanborn on Leadership

## Terry L. Paulson, Ph.D., CSP, CPAE

Dr. Terry Paulson is a licensed psychologist and author of the popular books, *They Shoot Managers Don't They, Secrets of Life Every Teen Needs to Know,* and *Making Humor Work.* His presentations empower leaders, employees and the next generation of American workers to make change work! He is past host of the ECI business television series entitled, "*Quality from the Human Side.*" His high-energy programs to such organizations as IBM, IMS, 3M, Merck, Nissan, Sears, and AHA are as entertaining as they are practical and timely. *Business Digest* has called him "the Will Rogers of management consultants." You'll understand after reading this book. For more information on his other books and his presentations, contact him directly at:

**Paulson and Associates, Inc.**
P.O. Box 365-POC
Agoura Hills, CA 91376-0365
818-991-5110
fax: 818-991-9648
online: drterryp@aol.com.